THE SOLDIER FACTORY

THE SOLDIER FACTORY

A Window

By Ed Salven

George Braziller Publishers

New York

First published in the United States of America in 2006 by
George Braziller, Inc.

Photographs of Fort Ord and of the paintings are by the author.

For information, please address the publisher:
George Braziller, Inc.
171 Madison Avenue
New York, NY 10016
www.georgebraziller.com

Library of Congress Cataloging-in-Publication Data:
Salven, Ed.
The soldier factory : a window / by Ed Salven.—1st ed.
p. cm.
ISBN-13: 978-0-8076-1572-0 (hardback)
ISBN-10: 0-8076-1572-2
1. Fort Ord (Calif.) 2. United States. Army—Military life. 3. Salven, Ed.
I. Title.
UA26.F675 .S36 2006
355.709794'76—dc22   2005037554

Designed by Saira Kathpalia
Printed and bound in Singapore
First edition

To Lawrence Walker of Atlanta

On July 16, 1968, I joined the millions of young men and boys who abruptly left behind their spoiled, self-indulgent lives as civilians and began their transformation inside the military. Having been drafted, I was inducted into the United States Army. I was twenty. My soldier factory was Fort Ord, a sprawling 1940s-era infantry base situated on the northern coast of California, overlooking beautiful Monterey Bay. In 1968 Ord was in high gear for war in Vietnam, as it had been during World War II and the Korean War. I soon became another cog in the great olive-drab machine that ceaselessly turned out men and material rain or shine, back in the days of "flower power" and "free love."

More than thirty years later, I again found myself in Monterey. Its compelling magic had crept into my soul. Over the decades I had been drawn back again and again to that beautiful and historic peninsula, yet never to the old fort itself. Steinbeck Country had captured my heart, as it had millions of hearts the world over. And so, one weekend in Monterey, on a getaway from smoggy Southern California, I was in my hotel room, and the thought came to me: I wonder what's happening at Fort Ord? Is it open? Closed? Still there? Gone? I didn't know it had been closed since 1994. I took a ten-minute drive to find out.

As I drove through the main entrance, past the empty guard shack and the tall naked flag pole onto the desolate grounds, a virtual torrent of distant sights, smells, emotions, and vivid memories rushed my senes. In stark contrast to my last stay, Fort Ord was now a ghost town—bowed fences, cracked concrete, sagging barracks, and a strange silence louder than sound.

It spoke to me.

I parked and took my bicycle from the truck, grabbed a pen and notepad, and began to pedal back through time. I wrote the text in a day and a night. Eighty-odd vignettes born in the past and resurrected in memory. The portraits (which are described in more detail on p. 159) I discovered on a subsequent visit. And I recognized instantly that these haunting faces were as much a part of the old fort as any other aspect. It was all GI.

The Soldier Factory is in a sense a tribute to the guys and gals I lived with, shared with, became friends with. Ordinary youth who had become icons in my mind's eye by our common experience. Everyone who has ever been in the military shares similar memories. Always unique to the individual, but common to all.

I called the work "A Window" because it's a view through time brought into sharp focus by truth and relevance. It's not my story, although I was a part of it. These writings are merely my observations as I sat at the window watching. Like film running slowly through a projector, scenes flashed before me frame by frame—indelible tableaux for us all to reflect on and file away in categories we must decide for ourselves. This book is therefore also dedicated to all those whose lives were forever altered by a soldier factory.

THE SOLDIER FACTORY

1

THE EMERALD CITY

Fort Ord is on the northern coast of California in Monterey.
Named after a Civil War general and built during World War II.
The fort will be torn down one day—maybe soon.
Whatever soon means in military time.
Now, in the new millennium, they're dismantling the rifle
ranges in the sand dunes along the shoreline, recontouring.
Making it appear as it was before the war. Wars.

In 1968 and '69 Fort Ord was a soldier factory, a city unto
itself.
An emerald city without the luster—green, olive drab.
The Sixth Army Infantry Processing Center.
It housed thirty thousand individuals.
Now it's a ghost town. Boarded up.
The homeless sleep outside its fences in the rain and cold.
Maybe they once slept inside its fences . . . Had been soldiers
made in that very factory a lifetime ago. Had been shipped
overseas to "The Nam" a lifetime ago. Had returned filled
with images that made the illusion of life outside of combat
meaningless, impossible to believe in or maintain—
Politics. Equity. Fairness. Job. Family. Pride. Love.
You had to apply for disability. A new battle. Another fight.
The war never ended.
Hearts filled with love and caring. Minds filled with faith
and hope.
Boarded up now. Vacant.

And the fate of the soldier is the same as the fate of the factory.

The rolling dunes will be wild and unblemished once more,

along the shore.

The only shrine is in the mind.

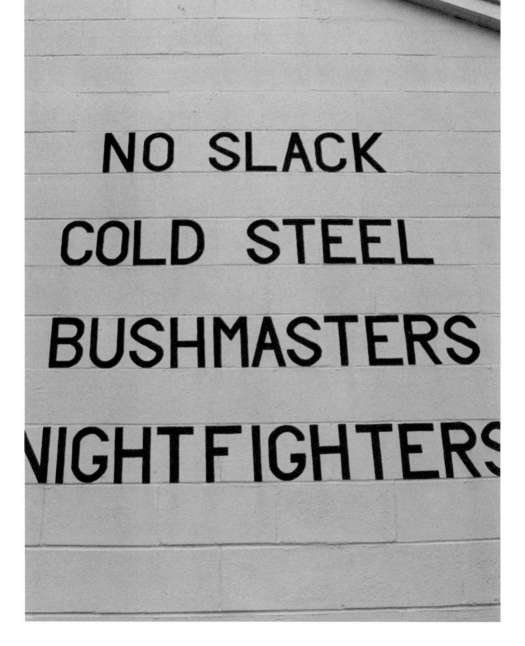

2

POPCORN

I fell asleep on the beach one day. It was summer, I think. I had my boots off, my shirt, too. My fatigue pants were rolled up to my knees.

It was warm.

The blue bay of Monterey lay to the south—Steinbeck country . . . Mack and the boys.

I was making dreams of civilian life. It was like a movie of wishes coming true, complete with popcorn popping.

Pop - Pop - Pop.

Pop - Pop - Pop.

The popcorn popping woke me up. I saw the sand around me popping, too. Like fleas dancing in the seaweed along the shore.

But too much sand was kicking up for fleas dancing, and the air was alive with the buzzing of metal bees, the whining of spiraling lead. Brass-jacketed M-16 rounds were humming just over my head, around me, past me, slashing into the ocean beside me.

I had fallen asleep below the rifle range. A fresh batch of new recruits had arrived. They were learning how to shoot silhouettes of people that symbolized an enemy half a world away, that they would engage someday soon.

Like the movie of a dream or a nightmare.

Complete with popcorn popping.

Pop - Pop - Pop.

Pop - Pop - Pop.

3

MAIL CALL

I had no idea the importance a piece of mail carried until
the Army.
Anticipation so thick you could run a bayonet through it. A
link as alive as fiber optics—
the CD-ROM of the human mind . . .
Wishes and dreams.
Digest the whole and fill in the blanks. Read between the
lines: entire novels.
Lives could turn on a dime inside a stamped envelope with an
APO[*] and a soldier's service number scrawled on the front.
Framed by red, white, and blue.
Love could reach out—be confirmed, be denied.
The classic Dear John turned killers into crybabies.

* *Army Post Office*

4

TOWN

We'd go into town—Monterey, Cannery Row, Carmel, Pacific Grove—in little bands or in pairs. In civilian life we'd never have hung together in a million years. But brought close, we were unified by the olive drab that digested everything and spat out soldiers.

Farm boys with hippies, Hawaiians with street-smart New Yorkers. Small brown guys from Guam sharing a pitcher of draft with a giant Swede from Iowa. A tattooed biker with a little Jewish guy who wanted to study law when he got out. Army buddies.

We'd put on disguises to go into town on a weekend pass—a crazy quilt of civilian clothes we thought would conceal our militariness. It was 1968 . . . paisleys and tie-dyes, bell-bottoms, fringes, beads, and leather. We'd wear all kinds of hats and stupid caps and bandannas, because we had no hair, when hair was king. We'd spend a good amount of time getting ready to go into town as civilians, forget the Army for a while. Get drunk. Eat pizza. Look at girls. Girls.

And when we finally got there, you could spot the young soldiers two city blocks away in their silly civvies with no hair, big ears, shiny black low quarters, and OD* green socks. Trying so hard.

* *Olive Drab*

5

BUMPER STICKER

Seen on many VW buses and bugs in 1968 and '69:

> Join the Army!
> Travel to far away lands.
> Meet exotic people.
> And kill them.

6

SONG

I want to be an airborne ranger—I want to live a life of danger.
I want to go to Vietnam—I want to kill old Charlie Cong.

7

THE MYTH

The myth of rank and medals made the impossible possible.

BARRACKS THIEF

There was a big poster just inside the barracks door, tacked to the wall. It read:

Beware the Barracks Thief!

It had a coiled rattlesnake on it, symbolizing the bite of the barracks thief. It went on to caution honest soldiers about the ways the barracks thief could, and would, prey on them. There were many ways.

Then one day the poster was gone. Only four thumbtacks remained.

The sergeant admonished and threatened, demanded to know where it went. Who took it?

But it seemed so obvious.

We all knew it could only have been . . .

SHOWERS

The walk-in showers in the company barracks had to pass inspection twice daily. They were tiled, of course, with several stainless-steel showerheads mounted above head level on one wall.

The inspecting officer or noncom would lay his cheek flat against the wall and stare down the lustrous surface, looking for any haze or flaw on the subatomic level. This was after the white-glove test.

Serious business they took seriously.

The walk-in showers couldn't have been cleaner.

And the acoustics were perfect for midnight jam sessions on the guitar and sing-alongs—folk music and antiwar songs that would have brought hard time in the stockade if anyone in charge ever heard them.

But no one who mattered ever did. And our white-tiled coffeehouse did booming after-hours business for a while, back in 1969.

·

10

109-B—LIGHT WEAPONS INFANTRY

A "grunt." Bad news when your orders were cut.

GIG LINE

Formation in the mornings was usually the standard boring bill of fare in the Receiving Company—being yelled at, because there was something wrong with your belt buckle that only the guy doing the yelling could see. Boots weren't shiny enough. Your "gig line" wasn't straight . . .

That was the imaginary vertical line that ran down the center of a soldier's uniform, from his cap, down the button line of his fatigue shirt, to his brass belt buckle, to the fly of his fatigue pants on down to the ground.

Things had to line up.

One morning, we had a new guy standing in formation. His fatigues were faded, worn. That mint green they got after time. The rank and unit patches on his shirt were sewn in black thread—SOP[*] in combat areas.

But this guy's gig line was perfect. It ran right down the center of his face like it was drawn with a ruler. The left side was tanned, clean shaven, though with the shadow of a beard. The skin on the right, however, was smooth and bright pink, stretched thin and almost white in places over the bone, like melted candle wax that had hardened again. The whole right side of his face had fallen a few inches. His right eye was gone. He had been the recipient of "friendly fire" in the form of napalm, the infamous incendiary jellied gasoline we dropped on the enemy over in The Nam.

A real bummer . . . but his gig line was straight.

* *Standard Operating Procedure*

US ARMY ABCs

ETA—MOS—ETS—PFC—KIA—DMZ.[*] Everything could be rendered into the essential initials.

---

[*] *Estimated Time of Arrival, Military Occupational Speciality, Estimated Time of Separation (from the Army), Private First Class, Killed in Action, Demilitarized Zone*

13

DISCHARGE

All sorts of people wanted out the moment they were in. Draftees, for the most part, but not exclusively. It didn't make much difference what you wanted.

But some guys got pretty creative in their methods of trying to get discharged early, under any discharge category. Private Preston, for example, staged realistic, hard-core, yet (according to him) phony homosexual encounters with another soldier, or soldiers, which he took Polaroid pictures of. Then he saw that the grainy, black-and-white photos reached the proper authorities. Creative.

After being propositioned by a high-ranking officer or two, which he spurned (according to him), he was discharged on a two-twelve, for convenience of the Army, within thirty days.

Another guy chanted his way out. To everyone's complete amazement, including the Army's. Na-mya-ho-ren-ge-kyo— Lemme outta here! Gone! True!

Private Walker, a black kid from Atlanta, Georgia, was an atheist, physicist, and conscientious objector. He objected to killing people, but didn't believe in any God or belong to any organized religion.

This, of course, was the criterion for applying for conscientious-objector status in the US Army.

A status that was routinely denied as soon as it was applied for.

Private Walker wrote his lengthy mathematical equation validating his belief that killing people was wrong. At least the way the Army was doing it over in Vietnam back in '68.

His petition was thick and very copious.

He was discharged ninety days later—honorably.

But the guy who was granted the most expedient exit from the Army was the guy who tore the fire ax off the barracks wall, shut himself in the sergeant's CQ* room, and threatened to chop to pieces anyone who tried to get him out.

Well, they got him out, somehow—and alive.

He was discharged that week on a Section 8, which I recall at the time confused us all to no end with the irony.

We all thought the guy was perfect soldier material—exactly what they were looking for.

* *Charge of Quarters*

14

THE ARs

Army regulations—volumes of big books, everything in
them—
The distance a brass buckle should be from a belt loop on
Class A trousers. The wattage of a front-porch lightbulb of
a noncom's house on base. The height of grass blades in all
lawns, in all forts anywhere. The distance your hand should
travel forward and backward, while marching.
If you ever wondered about anything, you didn't have to
worry, or even think . . .
It was somewhere in the ARs.

15

ARMY AXIOM

"Hurry up and wait!"

SHORT-TIMER

A "double-digit midget"—fewer than 100 days to ETS—
Estimated time of separation.

17

ARMY BASES

I only know the names of other US Army bases from the guys I knew at Ord, who were coming from and going to those bases. Some still stick in my mind, now almost mystical in memory—Arthurian, in a sense, from a time that has long since faded and blown away like tumbleweeds down the streets of a ghost town. And I wonder if tumbleweeds are blowing down the streets of those forts decaying across our nation, in the prevailing winds of budget cuts and a kind of disdain and political prejudice against our military different from that of 1968 and '69. Fort Leonard Wood, Missouri; Fort Bliss, Texas; Fort Benning, Georgia; Fort Lewis, Washington; in California, Fort Hunter-Liggett, Camp Roberts, the Presidio—names that conjured up images of familiarity, though I'd never been.

But how different could they be—in the transcendent continuity of the military?

Some of these places had pine trees around them. Others had cactus. Some had wheat or corn, some the ocean. But inside the fences, the olive drab gears turned the same, lubricated with the blood, sweat, and tears of the interchangeable parts that marched in rank and ran the machinery of war.

18

MOST-HEARD WORDS

On the battlefield after a battle: God . . . Mom . . . Medic.

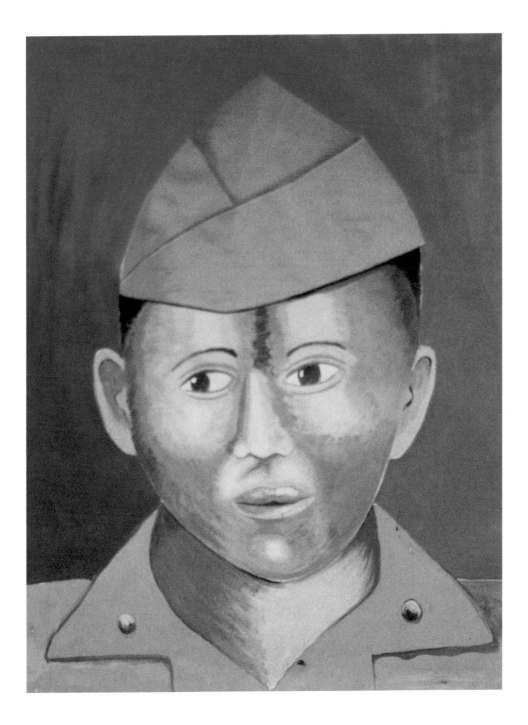

19

BARRACKS

The Army barracks were all the same, despite any differences.
The boards were covered with layers and layers of regulation
paint.

The floors were covered with layers and layers of regulation
wax.

And the whole thing was covered with layer upon layer of
regulations.

While as soldiers, we were exposed, stripped of our innocence, peevishness, and individuality. And what emerged was
our uniqueness and worth.

MEMORIES

Memories hurt in bittersweet clarity distorted by time.

But the tears are different in composition—desiccated by time.

Things I hated somehow made glorious now and valid by their mere existence.

By the fact that they came into being at all.

And that I experienced them.

The inexorable condition of our challenges: futility, grandeur.

Hugeness made miniature.

Smallness made vast.

The savage beauty of a lie made valuable beyond reason.

The reason we seek to believe.

The beliefs we die for.

The complex design of life, like the twisting steel of bedsprings on the bunk above.

An intricate pattern that means nothing, goes nowhere.

PLAYMATE

There was even a Playboy Playmate at Ord for a while—a centerfold.

Caprices of chance—thistles on the wind.

A blue-eyed rose among OD green thorns, living and breathing in the soldier factory in '69. She was the girlfriend of a soldier . . .

A draftee, of course.

They were bound together by civilian love.

Beatles and Stones.

She gave up the champagne and satin of the Hefner mansion. For a while . . .

They lived on Army food purloined from the officers' mess.

They slept under scratchy Army blankets stolen from the quartermaster.

She was the girlfriend of a soldier in '69. For a while.

But she was a Playboy Playmate—an anomaly. A hole in the fabric of a strange universe that began closing as soon as it had opened.

And then one day she was gone.

Olive drab was all that remained.

22

TET — 1 9 6 8

Chinese New Year.
Things we'd never heard of.
Things we'd never dreamed.

BREAKFAST

The Receiving Company was a transit company.
There were always new soldiers coming, going, waiting, processing.
The faces would change daily sometimes.

The new kids would wake up mornings in the barracks on the north coast of California, get dressed, pull on socks and boots.
They'd polish and buff, swap stories of battles they'd fought mere hours ago . . . Gun barrels melting down—hand to hand.

The kids would show off battle souvenirs: fatigue shirts with holes in them that they were wearing when bullets passed right through the folds.

The kids would smile a knowing smile to each other, look with knowing eyes of men who'd been in combat. They spoke in low tones.
They'd finish dressing, then go off to breakfast.

BATTLEFIELD AXIOM IN 1968 AND '69

"Don't mean nothin'!"

THE BOYS ARRIVED

The boys arrived, draftees and gung ho alike.

Two years and four years.

US and RA.[*]

Defiant and compliant.

But soon even their birthmarks seemed to fade away, as the green olive drab consumed them.

---

* *United States, as in the drafted forces, and Regular Army, the volunteer, or enlisted, forces*

CAVEMAN

We were standing in the white-tiled showers one evening, in a warm sudsy lather—the first protocol of getting "squared away" to go into town and look at people who weren't in the Army.

Suddenly, a young, skin-headed soldier ran right into our shower, in fatigues and jump boots. He stood flat against the short, right-angled wall that enclosed the showers from the rest of the latrine. He was getting all wet and hyperventilating. He just stared at us. And we stared back. He had a dark blue tattoo on his neck. It read: Caveman.

A moment later a short, stocky MP[*] burst into the latrine. A long wooden GI[†] nightstick in his left hand, a .45 pistol in his right. His face was blood red, and his eyes were filled with murder. He glanced quickly around the small room, at the five toilets sitting side-by-side, bolted to the floor, no panels or doors to separate them, at the three naked soldiers standing side-by-side under the showerheads, looking back at him.

"Did anyone see a prisoner run through here?" the MP shouted at us.

We looked back at him through the spray, then at the soaked soldier trembling behind the white-tiled wall, then back at the MP. We all shook our heads in unison: No!

The MP ran to the open window, past the row of

* Military Policeman
† Government Issue

sinks and mirrors, and looked outside the barracks in both directions, then up and down. Then he leaned back inside and brought his billy club down so hard on the windowsill that it broke in two. He ran out cursing and swearing, holding only his .45.

Later that night, two GIs on a weekend pass took Caveman back to his cave down in LA.

THE OFFICERS' MESS

The officers' mess hall in the Hospital Company was like the Hilton Hotel's brunch buffet compared to the normal enlisted men's mess halls, whose sergeants took a creative approach to preparing the almost-food served there, breakfast, lunch, and supper.

For example: One big, fat, E-6 mess sergeant invented boiled pork roast with peanut butter sauce and a side dish of hearty, 50/50 mashed potatoes—50 percent spuds and 50 percent lard. A soup spoon could be stuck into them at a 45-degree angle forever, without falling.

Or the timeless classic SOS (shit-on-a-shingle). Creamed chipped beef on toast. It was never conclusive that the beef was beef, or the toast was toast.

Or eggs that would drive off wild coyotes in the mornings. Powdered eggs. From a box!

But the officers' mess had food. Even salad. Like on Earth. Fresh greens, and not OD. And dress greens weren't required to get in.

What was required was a rectangle of pink blotter paper about three by four inches with special words printed on it, saying that the cardholder was special, that he (or she) was an officer.

Not many "shes" back then, except nurses.

So, for about fifteen cents' worth of pink blotter paper from a stationery store in Pacific Grove, we became mealtime officers—wore civvies—clothes nonmilitary, that any hip person back in '69 wouldn't have used, not even as rags to wash their car . . . Sta-Prest shirts, stupid straight-legged slacks, in a time of bell-bottoms only, please. But there we were, sitting shoulder to shoulder with the elite, eating their food, trying to imagine what in the world they were thinking.

They were officers. We were not.

SERGEANT E-6 FRANKLIN

Sergeant Franklin had won everything but the Medal of Honor by the time he was nineteen in Vietnam. He'd enlisted when he was seventeen with a parental note of consent. Conditionally.

The condition being that Private E-1 Franklin be stationed in Germany for his tour of duty, to avoid the unpleasantness of South Vietnam, which was not a tourist destination at the time. The Army agreed, and he enlisted for four years. After his BCT and AIT,* he spent thirteen months in Germany. Good duty.

But Private Franklin hadn't read the fine print.

He was in Vietnam shortly after his eighteenth birthday.

That year he would survive an enemy ambush in which he took command of what remained of his platoon, was wounded twice, was awarded the Bronze Star, was awarded the Silver Star, was awarded the Purple Heart with clusters, and more . . .

He was promoted in rank to sergeant first class.

He became a "tunnel runner"—seeking out the subterranean enemy, with only a flashlight and a .45.

We became friends in 1969, in Fort Ord.

We'd get stoned. Drink beer in the pizza joints on Cannery Row.

* *Basic Combat Training and Advanced Individual Training*

And he'd describe macabre tableaux of death he could recall from his visit to Vietnam as a teenager—a VC's[†] body, bouncing lifeless over the tops of tall trees, coaxed by the hammering fire from a .50-caliber machine gun mounted on the back of a jeep. Faces he'd never forget. Eyes. Pieces of people.

He'd been born and raised in Lodi, central California—a nondescript agricultural town cleaved by Highway 99 and studded with the ubiquitous coffee shops and family restaurants that came and went like the parasitic businesses that surround military bases.

Sergeant E-6 Franklin enlisted at seventeen with a note of parental consent (his mother's) to get away from an abusive stepfather. But he had had no idea what abuse his Uncle had in store.

† *Viet Cong*

29

JOHN STEINBECK

John Steinbeck was born in Salinas, California, in 1902. Back then it was a small agricultural town with a large immigrant population, whose various ethnic backgrounds were made well known in his novels—*Tortilla Flat, The Grapes of Wrath, Cannery Row, East of Eden.*

Steinbeck died in 1968 when many descendants of those immigrants he wrote of resided in Fort Ord—or had at least passed through the Sixth Army Infantry processing factory in their metamorphosis from civilian to soldier.

At night, the lights of Salinas lay far below the East Garrison on the same rolling dunes covered in ice plants and low flowering brush as the rest of the fort. But the East Garrison was vacant, except for some old sun-bleached, boarded-up barracks with peeling paint and bowed siding that were used to store stuff the Army rarely needed in 1968 and '69.

They used to store Japanese people in them, back in 1942, when the internment was in force.

But in 1968 and '69 the East Garrison was pretty much used only by soldiers who would sneak off into the dunes at night to smoke weed, take acid, and trip out on the colorful lights of Salinas that lay strewn across the long valley far below.

30

CHARLIE

It was a big tumorlike thing, about the size of a Concord grape, the same color, too, on the inside of his lower lip. His name was Charlie. (Just one of the many slurs we used for the enemy over in Vietnam back then: Charlie—Gook—Dink—Zipper-head—Slope.)

Charlie was a nineteen-year-old door-gunner on a Huey chopper that patrolled the Central Highlands and the river deltas of South Vietnam, back in 1967 and '68. He manned a belt-fed .50 caliber on a turret.

Whenever he encountered suspected enemy on the ground far below him and fired on them, he bit his lower lip almost all the way through—tasted blood as he watched the bodies below him shatter to pieces under the murderous hailstorm of lead he was ordered to unleash.

31

CLIPBOARD

A clipboard and an attitude would gain you access to any restricted area on the base. Restricted areas were usually manned by sentries.

Being a sentry was bad duty. Usually the lowest of the low drew the chore, no matter how restricted the area.

Private E-1s or E-2s.

They stood like Beefeaters, straight and tall outside a door or a gate.

Sometimes they were given rifles to hold.

Their sole purpose in life was to restrict access to "unauthorized personnel."

Two big words for big-eared kids who had failed finger painting in kindergarten.

The clipboard represented purpose—a cause under color of authority.

A blank piece of paper was a real edge. Or any scrap with printing on it.

It was transformed by the clipboard into a document—a tangible order made manifest by someone, somewhere.

Orders could be countermanded—superseded. New orders could be cut.

Orders were often nebulous, confusing.

Orders were almost from a different dimension. Like hollow, distant echoes reverberating down from the clouds surrounding Mount Olympus.

They could result in thunder, lightning, even death.

Attitude was necessary to break down the defenses of a sentry.
It was easy.
The defenses of a sentry were a house of cards. They were following orders, after all.
It was imperative that you spoke nonsense loudly and, with conviction mixed with trepidation, brandished the clipboard and cited rank:
"Colonel Leydencrayden needs lederhosen by o-nine hundred, or it's gonna be maydenpayden!"
And you had to keep advancing—he could shoot, but you'd die inside the restricted area.
The "open sesame" of the US Army.

DON'T ASK — DON'T TELL

Sergeant Campbell had a piece of corkscrew shrapnel wind-
ing through his spine.
A souvenir of the Central Highlands.
But that wasn't his greatest pain.

PRIVATE BREWER

Private Brewer was a black street kid from Chicago—broken
home, part-time pimp, occasional drug dealer, good heart.
But the worst thing was, he couldn't obey orders. Always went
AWOL.* Always got caught.

Finally, one morning, the Chi-town FBI broke in his door
at 6:00 a.m.—kicked the girl out and took him in.

They returned him to the nearest Army post.

He was given a choice: finish out his eighteen-month tour in
Japan or do twice that time in Leavenworth, Kansas. There
was a federal prison there, round and old.

It was a bummer there.

Being street-smart, he took Japan.

He thought the flight would be direct.

When his plane landed, Private Brewer stepped out onto the
tarmac in South Vietnam. Someone shoved an M-60 machine gun into his hands (a weapon he'd never been trained
on) and told him, "You can go AWOL anywhere you want
now, nigger!"

Private Brewer was hit his first day out in the bush, on his
first patrol. AK-47 rounds—three of them, up his left side.
Never knew what hit him. He woke up in a morphine dream
in a hospital in Japan.

The Army had fulfilled their part of the bargain.

* *Absent Without Leave*

Three days later he was back in Fort Ord. New cane, plastic prosthesis, and a few kilos of Thai weed smuggled in and stashed off-base. He was looking forward to slipping away into the dunes above the rifle ranges or to the East Garrison, kicking back with a nice Thai stick and a cold Budweiser—dreaming about civilian life again. He'd just have to make three o'clock formation . . .

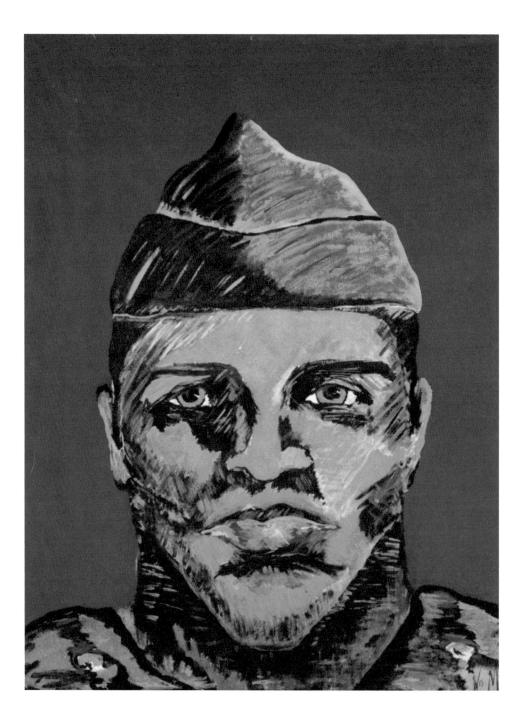

34

W I N D O W S I L L

I was sitting in the window of my barracks one day, as a line
of boot-camp grunts ran by below me, following a DI[*] in
a Smoky-the-Bear hat, brass whistle on a brass chain, the
whole bit.
They were stomping by in cadence.

They were singing death songs, of course.

It was a long line. Took a long time to go by. So I had a
long time to bring the ordinary into focus. It interrupted my
thoughts of civilian life and what was going on out in "The
Real World."

I started staring at the soldiers stomping by below me . . .
Skinheads, big red ears, eyes on the back of the next one in
line—
Manufacturing their mettle from the sameness of those
around them.

It suddenly hit me: The Army, this Army, the real Army was
nothing like the one I grew up with on TV or in the movies,
where tough-as-nails grown men kicked ass on the enemies
of the United States—Krauts, Japs, dirty Commies. World
War II, Korea. Guys like Robert Ryan, Randolph Scott, John
Wayne, of course, Jack Palance, Vic Morrow. Even Audie

* *Drill Instructor*

Murphy playing himself wasn't quite right; he was too cute.

But sitting on the barracks windowsill, I suddenly realized the real Army was an Army of children—kids in uniform.

The grown-ups were somewhere off-base, thinking up catch-phrases and just causes, lyrics to death songs and budgets. What it would cost to keep the gears turning on the grinder.

35

RECEIVING COMPANY REPRISE

The Receiving Company was a transit company, where soldiers came and went from almost anywhere to somewhere else. For all sorts of reasons.

Guys pretending to be homosexuals, processing out "for the convenience of the Army."

Farm boys from the Midwest, who kept photos of their tractors in their wallets instead of photos of girls.

There were returning combat vets, who kept photos of dead people in their wallets—VC they'd killed. Little skinny guys, sitting slumped on the ground. Posed for the camera on blood-stained dirt half a world away with bamboo sticks shoved up nostrils, kicked up into their brains by kids who would go back to work in shoe stores, fast-food places, gas stations in a matter of months, weeks, days, hours.

You could wake up to almost anyone in the next bunk over, in the bunk above or below, in the Receiving Company back in 1968 and '69.

36

THE HOSPITAL

The hospital in Fort Ord would fill up seventy-two hours after major battles in Vietnam, like clockwork. First you would hear about it on the radio, then read about it in the post paper or in the *Stars & Stripes* the next day.

On the third day, the boys would start to arrive.

It was trickle-down economics with a different spin.

From the battlefield MASH[*] units in Vietnam, the wounded and grave casualties would be shipped out to US Army hospitals in Japan. When these were filled to capacity, the wounded would be sent to Fort Lewis, Washington. After filling that to capacity, they were rotated to Fort Ord in Monterey, California. If capacity was reached in Ord's hospital, they would filter down to Fort Mac in LA.

Only hours before, the heroic young men from across America had faced fear they couldn't have dreamed of—discovered the meaning of bravery and sacrifice the rhetoric of ten thousand college courses could never impart.

And the doctors and nurses who treated them, put them back together, cut them apart discovered an aspect to their oath and practice they had never dreamed of in civilian life.

Maybe there was no meaning—but it was reciprocal, self-fulfilled in action.

[*] *Mobile Army Surgical Hospital*

37

THE HOUSE ON LA SALLE STREET

In Seaside was our Shangri-La for a while—a little parasitic town of hookers and bars, of liquor stores, gas stations,
and auto-parts stores that depended on the fort for its life's
blood.

Seaside was born in the 1940s during World War II, when
the little clapboard house was built. The yard was sand and
ice plants and the tough-as-nails coastal stuff that depended
on nothing to exist.

Inside the tiny house was a space station. An oasis of marijuana smoke, Nag Champa incense, baking bread, Indian
brass stuff, paisley cloth hanging on walls. And music on the
hi-fi record player (big black LPs): Hendrix, Joplin, Doors,
Dylan. Jazz. Or "It's Your Thing!" by the Isley Brothers.
"Time" by the Chambers Brothers. The same sounds mov-
iemakers put in movies, decades later, to define the time.

We'd sit on the old sofa and matching chair, both spewing
stuffing from their arms and cushions. We'd lie on blue-
and-white-striped Army mattresses and philosophize, listen
to music.

We'd smoke and drink.

Wearing our fatigues, our boots in a pile on the hardwood
floor.

We'd kick back. But there was no escape.

We were soldiers, as much as we didn't want to admit it.

PILLS FOR PORN

Staff Sergeant E-6 Candy worked in the Fort Ord Hospital
Company pharmacy in 1969.

She wore crisp, starched fatigues. Was short, dark, burly.

A lesbian from somewhere in the Bible Belt.

E-6 Candy wanted skin rags from the porn stands in Marina,
a small town north of the fort.

But she was shy. Too embarrassed to buy them.

We weren't.

We wanted to get up, get down, when we went into town.

Staff Sergeant E-6 Candy worked in the pharmacy.

So we traded . . .

Pills for porn.

PRIVATE LOCKE'S CAR

Private Locke's car was a symbol of freedom—a vehicle to an ideal of freedom in town.

A shuttle craft to the void, where you could walk around with your hands in your pockets, with your buttons unbuttoned, your cap off.

Monterey being the void of choice. Cannery Row. The Wharf.

It was a 1959 Ford Fairlane four-door with no seats, just lots of scratchy Army blankets piled on the bare coiled springs front and back. The floor looked like you were outside somewhere, anywhere in a city.

It was flat blue with some remaining chrome trim that had not been torn off. It had no radio, of course—but it got pretty good mileage.

That wasn't the problem.

It drank a quart of oil every two miles.

The oil light would turn on like clockwork every two miles.

The soldiers in the car had to be combat ready with their open cans of oil so the engine wouldn't blow on their way to freedom or back from it.

But even though every quart of oil meant one less quart of beer, it was worth it.

And the old blue Ford might have been a showroom-new Caddy for all we cared.

THE MAGIC OF FLIGHT

Just a few weeks before, Specialist 5 Giamilla woke up in tall elephant grass with his intestines in a green and blue pile beside him. He gathered them up and put them back into his belly where they belonged.

Then he walked back to his lines in South Vietnam.
They gave him medals for doing this.
He deserved them.

On one clear evening back in Ord, Spec 5 Giamilla was smoking marijuana in the remote dunes of the East Garrison, overlooking the colorful city lights of Salinas. Home sweet home.

He hadn't been back that long, and his stomach still hurt. But it was the weed with roots in hell. And they caught him. His court martial resulted in six months in the stockade.

41

ESPERANTO

The signs are slowly changing around the grand old fort in the new millennium. It's now at the same crossroads of relative reality as Einstein's equations, where physics meets metaphysics, where numbers and letters turn into particles of light beaming back to their sources. Even now the ubiquitous stenciled Army acronyms are peeling off, flaking away— paint chips, like snowflakes, ride the winds of change across the beautiful blue bay.

In their place another form of communication is revealed . . . written in a mysterious language, it poses a cosmic question wrapped in a riddle inside an enigma. It could be in a span of fallen chain link, imprinting its oxidized design on cracked concrete of the desolate parade grounds. It could be the twisted boughs of a long dead Monterey cypress, casting its spent life force as a shadow across the wall of a sagging barracks. Or in the golden wood grain and bleeding knots on a sheet of plywood nailed up as a barrier over a door or a window. Any or all of these things and countless more could hold a message, even knowledge if we would see it.

Our alphabet is simply angles and curves we fashion into letters and combine to form words. Inadequate tools we use inadequately to convey our feelings, ideas, emotions, our wants and needs. But these recognizable designs of communication are no less arcane than myriad other angles and curves, organic and manmade, which naturally combine throughout time to form an alphabet of their own, one no less valid than any other. And no more obtuse, if one cannot read or divine its angles and curves.

And could it not be that surf sounds, their familiar rushing whisper along the shore below the rifle ranges, are an endless tattoo of admonishment, or of direction, or solution? If only we would hear. If only we would listen. Perhaps this is the one language, the only truly universal and common language we all must learn to finally live in peace and brotherhood the world over.

42

BRIDGE

I remember the chain link fence around the fort could have been a thousand feet high, and the highway, US Highway 1, could have been the canals of Mars, so inaccessible were they most of the time.

A long concrete bridge spanned the civilian highway, connecting the fort to Stilwell Hall on the dunes above the rifle ranges—a recreational facility named after a World War I general. Nobody really went, because you couldn't drink beer there. Everyone went into town. Stilwell Hall pretty much stayed empty.

One day there was a buzz of news—there'd been flashing lights on the highway below the bridge. Someone heard that there'd been an accident, a bad one, and it involved a soldier. It was true.

The kid had just returned the day before from a thirteen-month tour of combat duty in Vietnam. He'd been wounded, decorated. He'd faced death every day and every night, every minute, while in-country.

And then he was killed turning onto the highway outside the fort, heading to Monterey.

43

DESIGN

The Hospital Company at Fort Ord was unique, in a way,
from other stateside posts. Built during World War II, it
was designed like a checkerboard and covered several square
acres. The long wards and long covered ramps that con-
nected them ran along the lines of the checkerboard—and
inside the large squares was "dead space," filled with sand
and the ubiquitous ice plants. This design was meant to mit-
igate casualties in the Hospital Company, should the Japanese bombers breach our coastal defenses. The only time a
breach had occurred was up north in San Francisco, when
a Japanese submarine shot a torpedo at a fishing boat and
missed. It hit a truck on shore.

But the hospital's design was still a good one.

44

THE "CAUSE"

They could sell it, but never fully explain it.

45

ITALIAN VILLA

The door to the mess hall was like a door to a different dimension where time stood still for a while.
You would be left alone while you ate.
Not completely, but it felt like a break.
That was, unless you had KP.*
Then you became one of several things: Back Porch Man—bad!
The job was continuously depositing leftover slop into various metal trash cans, making on-the-spot decisions. Was it fat? Grease? Meat of some kind? Liquid? What?
Or, Pot & Pan Man—bad! For obvious reasons.
Server—good!
DRO—Dining Room Orderly—good! A skate!

The Receiving Company's mess hall was romantically called "The Italian Villa." It had a small wood sign above the entrance and bunches of nonregulation plastic grapes hanging here and there from the rafters inside.
Of course, like all other mess halls in Fort Ord and all other US Army forts across America, we threw out enough perfectly good food every single meal, three times a day, every day, to feed entire towns.
It went to the dump.
Well, not all of it.
Some of the good, uncooked, USDA Grade A meats and

* *Kitchen Police*

unopened canned goods, sauces, and seasonings, rolls and breads went into the trunk of the mess sergeant's blue Chevy Bel Air, to be driven into Salinas, where he owned a family restaurant romantically called "The Italian Villa."

46

S W A N   D I V E

A kid tried to commit suicide one night.

He jumped out a second-story barracks window.

But he landed on two MPs on fire watch.

They thought they were being jumped.

Beat the kid with nightsticks so badly he almost died in the hospital.

When the truth got out, the kid was charged with trying to destroy government property.

He was Government Issue: GI.

The kid was court-martialed and got time in the stockade.

LIEUTENANT CHEETO

You salute the rank, not the man. Military axiom.

We were kids, really: 18–19–20–21. Full of mischief and folly that was nonlethal stateside but could be channeled destructively.

One day we were cruising around the fort in Private Jensen's powder-blue VW bug, listening to the radio.

We were drinking beer from cans, eating Cheetos from a big bag.

We wore fatigues, of course.

After a six-pack or two, it occurred to us that a Cheeto (a crunchy orange squiggle of fried cheddar cheese and flour) looked remarkably like the gold bar of a second lieutenant, especially if chewed into shape.

By piercing a Cheeto with a straight pin and fixing it to the front of my beat-up fatigue cap, I awarded myself a field commission and became a second lieutenant in the United States Army.

Lieutenant Cheeto.

Enlisted men and noncoms on every corner snapped to and saluted me.

And I saluted back.

Until we all grew bored.

I ate my rank and washed it down with cold beer.

You salute the rank, not the man.

FORT ORD'S STOCKADE

Fort Ord's stockade was kind of the flip side of a civilian jail, nonviolent offenders mostly—drunks who went AWOL by mistake. Soldiers caught with drugs, of course.

A kid tried to escape one day. He had no prior practice.
Climbing the tall chain link and razor wire fence, he was shot in the back.
His executioner wore the same uniform, was about the same age.
As SOP, he was given a pack of cigarettes and a transfer to a new Army post. The cost of the spent cartridge was deducted from the executioner's pay—fifty cents.
Standard operating procedure.

We were in the Army to learn how to kill or support it.
Not be punished for it. It was a dubious crowd.

The dead kid's mother started an organization for "Soldiers' Rights."
It died, too.

BUS RIDE

I took the drive up from the LA Induction Center on a bus bound for Fort Ord with a few dozen other draftees, including a few big, scary-looking bikers. They wore standard biker gear: greasy denim embroidered with names and places, silver stuff—skulls, big rings, earrings, black boots with straps and buckles. They all had beards and mustaches, lots of tattoos.

Hell's Angels types. Ass-kickin' troublemakers on wheels. Well, once on wheels.

Now on US Army wheels, in an OD green bus, rolling toward their new home.

The Army was even bigger and scarier than the bikers.
It was ready and waiting.
In 1968 it had been ready for almost two hundred years.
The soldier factory was in full operation.
Capacity quotas met with ease—relative ease.
The Sixth Army Infantry.

The Army swallowed the bikers whole. Digested them in hours.

Ran them through the production line without a hitch: Denim and silver gone. Fatigues on. Cycle boots gone. Jump

boots on. A barber-shop stop—hair and beards gone. Regulation cue-ball look on. They all looked like cats dipped into a swimming pool when they got spit out.

I recognized the skinny white guys only by their scary-looking tattoos in the showers we took before morning formation.

50

RECORD PLAYER

We'd listen to the new Bob Dylan album, *Nashville Skyline*, on the record player in the chaplain's office, over and over, when he was out.

"Lay Lady Lay."

The chaplain was a light colonel—a man of God.

He'd been to Vietnam, had 8 x 10 photos behind glass in frames on his wall—of him, with the troops. Silver cross on one collar, silver oak leaf on the other.

The photos were in black and white but could not disguise the OD green of everything caught by the lens.

The young boys were smiling up at the colonel—looking for answers with dark beseeching eyes as big as dimes. Looking for absolution or forgiveness.

But for answers, most of all.

Even we wondered how he resolved "Thou Shalt Not Kill" for the troops. There was no fine print in the Bible. But we never asked him.

We just listened to Dylan's "Lay Lady Lay" on his record player, over and over again.

51

CHURCH SERVICE

This is the roof—this is the steeple. Open it up, and see all the people . . . A kid's game played with enmeshed fingers.

It conjures up memories of two MPs escorting a black prisoner across the base one sunny day. He was between them; each held an arm, firmly.

The prisoner was squirming, kicking, struggling. He was swearing profanely. He was not acknowledging the exalted rank and position of his tormentors. He kept yelling: "I know my rights!"
They were passing a small white church, with the classic tall steeple in front.

It was midday—midweek. The congregation of soldiers wasn't in.
Neither was the chaplain.
The church was empty.

The MPs made an on-the-spot decision American soldiers are so renowned for. Independent thinking within the ranks.

They took their prisoner into the empty church, kicking and screaming, taking the Lord's name in vain. Minutes later, the three emerged in the same configuration—each MP gripping an arm, holding up their prisoner as they walked him across the baking blacktop, boots dragging, scuffing, his head down, blood flowing down his chin onto his fatigue jacket.

He was out cold—silent as the space between mortar rounds. Dreaming of his rights.

BEACH

Fort Ord was like all US Army bases in most ways, but remarkable for one, I recall. It was bordered on the west by beaches and breaking waves. You could easily tell it was military property because most of the shells on the beach were brass.

If you walked north, along the shoreline, past the rifle ranges up on the dunes, you would soon encounter dead seals and sea lions, pelicans and gulls, cormorants and egrets that had died of lead poisoning. The same kind of lead poisoning that was killing people by the thousands over in Vietnam.

The off-duty soldiers would walk up the beach, drinking 3.2 beer, carrying M-16s or M-60s, .45s or shotguns. They'd kill anything that moved or didn't move, that swam or flew. This activity wasn't even frowned upon, really. It was only practice, and they were only animals, after all. It was 1968—before the heyday of Greenpeace and PETA—before protesters would die for a spotted owl or kangaroo rat, a dolphin or a whale.

All the better, really, because if protestors had been around then, when you walked the shoreline past the rifle ranges of Fort Ord back in 1968 or '69, there would have been dead seals and sea lions, gulls, and Greenpeace people lying there. It was only practice for the "real thing" over in The Nam.

GODS

Second Lieutenant — First Lieutenant — Captain — Major —
Light Colonel — Full Bird — the lofty levels of General.

Gods in OD green held the power of life and death, looking
down from above.

DOUGHBOY THEATER

Fort Ord's movie house. Wood siding painted OD green—
no frills.

The marquee was set in big red plastic letters.

One day it read: JOHN WAYNE—THE GREEN BERETS.

Some considered this a mind-altering event back then—having real soldiers sitting in a dark bungalow, eating popcorn,
Milk Duds, Hershey's Kisses, watching fake soldiers die on
the silver screen, depicting a real war, really going on.

A war they might be on their way to, or returning from.

It just didn't seem fair, even economically.

The base pay of a real soldier, private E-1, was, at the time,
$125 per month with a bump for hazardous duty in a com-
bat zone.

The base pay of a Hollywood movie actor was about $200
per day and a box lunch, with a bump for meal penalties
and overtime.

Truly psychedelic in the days of flower power and napalm in
1968 and '69.

55

MIRAGE

Maybe it's only an ideal.
Maybe it will never be real.
Or never has been.
But maybe if we stop butchering our youth—
Stop shedding their blood for it.
The world would be worse.
Maybe dying for a mirage is better than dying for a desert.

56

M O S

If you were a four-star chef in civilian life, the Army put you to work in the motor pool. If you knew a lot about car engines, you went to work in the laundry. If you couldn't boil water or toast bread, you became a mess sergeant.
Everyone knew that. That's just the way it was.

REVEILLE

The reveille was on a record, black vinyl. I always got a kick
out of that.
Some old, scratchy LP over the PA in the mornings.
Like a rubber rooster, sounding off at first light.
At the height of the Vietnam War.
You'd think they could have dug up some boogie-woogie
bugle boy from Company B to blow a real brass horn for
the troops.
I mean it's tradition, right?
But he was probably a cook in some mess hall somewhere.

58

PATCHES AND PINS

One Hundred and First Airborne Division—Screaming Eagles.
Eighty-Second Airborne, Queen of Battle—vertical broad-
blade sword.
First Cavalry—big yellow patch, diagonal black line and
horse's head.
First Infantry Division—The Big Red One.
Artillery—crossed cannons.
Infantry—silver rifle on a blue rectangle.
Airborne soldier—winged parachute.
Pins and patches—symbols and logos imprinted on my mind.
A direct line to the past, into history bathed in blood, forged
and tempered in blood. Made iron-hard by the glory of battle.
Self-sacrifice supreme.
Homage to brave young men of the very same units who
overcame their fear, faced death, meted out death, gave their
all in other wars to preserve and defend ideals, rights—our
very lives.
Young men, who answered the call, became soldiers—who
brought their naïveté and wide-eyed innocence to the battlefield, became the pieces on the checkerboard of politics.
Brave young men who gave old, flaccid hypocrites and arm-
chair cowards their indignant thunder and accusatory fire,
spewed so eloquently out of harm's way.
Brave young soldiers who turned their childhood hopes and
dreams of brotherhood and humanity into swift and merciless
death, to preserve whatever it is that makes life worth living.

Add shine and luster to the grand illusion. Safeguard love.
Young brave soldiers who grew old—lived out their lives as
broken and incomplete parts in small drab rooms, contem-
plating the grandest riddle that bridged eternity.

Old men bathed in tears of a memory half a century old,
yet crystal in clarity. Painful as a honed blade turning. Loss.
Love. Friendship. Macabre horror. Need.

The need to believe it has meaning beyond the symbols of
patches and pins.

59

EX-PRESIDENT

General of the Army, Dwight David Eisenhower, died in 1969.
They shot big howitzers into the sky at Fort Ord in his honor.
Blank 105s—powder charges with no shells.
They thundered over the bay.
There was silence about the ex-president's view on the war
in Vietnam.
But it was widely known that he, as a military man, opposed it.

CAPTAIN TATE

From the heart of Dixie—military family for generations.

Two tours in Vietnam—Purple Heart—Steel heel.

He loved "Poke Salad Annie" on AM radio—

Reminded him of home.

He loved the Army.

Loved it.

Got a haircut every seventy-two hours. His scalp was raw from the barber's shears.

Loved to wear his dress greens into town. His Class A hat, with the gold braid on the brim we called "Scrambled Eggs."

He'd strut past the hippies in Carmel like a fighting cock with a silver spur.

Razor creases and gleaming brass, cleaving paisley and tie-dye with pride.

He'd entered the Army as an enlisted man—had gone to night school between battles to get commissioned, had become an officer, had elevated his status.

He thought the war in Vietnam was bullshit—all the way.

He knew America was bigger.

He loved America.

Loved it.

61

FALL

Olive drab, serpentine waves of youth, stomping in line,
singing, shouting death songs below my barracks window—
A forever tableau.
Foggy breath—no hair—big red ears in the fall cold.
Babes.
Caught in the jaws of a cause.
Chewed up and spit out.
Winter just around the corner.

62

DOWN THE DRAIN

A teenager sat on the floor of the tiled shower, naked, alone.
Would-be warrior.
Blood flowed from his wrists—a blue plastic Gillette razor
between his knees.
He couldn't be a soldier—couldn't understand going to a
foreign land to kill an unknown man.
He could kill . . .
But not another.

63

RADIO

Was like getting away—or at least getting away with something.
Music. Rock & Roll. Pop. R & B. The psychedelic stuff.
Everyone would mix it up—act silly, like girls at a high school
dance party.

Then Eldridge Cleaver's book *Soul on Ice* came out . . .
And all the blacks danced on one end of the barracks.

MORE MAGIC OF FLIGHT

Some returned shell-shocked, awestruck, that quiet.

Only hours before, their best friends had stared at them with lifeless eyes.

Now, just outside the chain link fence, traffic lights directed their lives.

Cars honked at each other.

People around them complained about petty and ridiculous things again.

WEEKEND PASS

Thumbs up!
Most soldiers didn't have cars, couldn't afford cabs, and buses
didn't go to cool places . . . So we'd hitchhike—thumbs up!
Half a day in the blazing sun on an on-ramp somewhere.
You'd stand on a foggy moonlit corner in the middle of no-
where, frozen to the bone, for twelve hours, to spend six at your
destination—then turn right around and make formation.
Monday morning, o-six hundred hours.

REHAB WARD

US Army Hospital Company, Fort Ord, California—1969.
Pretzel boys—GI toys.
Crazy angles—limbs bent—gone.
Plastic and stainless steel.
Slings and traction.
Shadows of night stretch across the day, through tall, paned
windows looking out on forever.
Sundown.
Night sounds: Prayers and laments, sobs muffled by an
Army pillow.
Sunrise.
A twinkling eye, fire of hope, smiling out from bloody gauze.

67

TIME

The Army kind—the 24-hour clock.

O-nine hundred hours was also 21 hundred hours.

One was day—one was night.

Confusing at first, but then a piece of cake.

And as accurate as an hourglass full of sand from the rifle-

range dunes.

68

ALARM CLOCK

Pretty basic design.
But effective.
A soup ladle banged nonstop inside an empty tureen, held
six inches (or less) from the ear of a sleeping soldier.
"Drop your cocks and grab your socks, it's morning, ladies!"

69

K I D S

I used to look at these kids sometimes—the returning combat vets.

A side-glance prolonged by their enigmatic difference.

I was a kid, too, wore the same clothes.

They were my age.

But different.

There's a disease. I don't know its name, but it makes kids
old—look old.

Ages them years ahead of schedule.

Then they die young.

But old, too.

Combat is like that disease.

The kids looked old. Their eyes were old—lackluster.

It turned a smile into a grimace.

Their experience in Vietnam had killed their childhood.

Aged them years ahead of schedule.

And many did, and would, die young.

GI

I was from So-Cal, so I took a lot for granted.

Like being able to read and write. Knowing how to use a toothbrush—soap.

Some of that was covered in orientation the first week in the Reception Company, the rest in Basic Combat Training—BCT. They couldn't teach you to read and write in eight weeks, but as an infantry grunt, you had to recognize certain signs, some words, colors and symbols, a few numbers.

What wasn't covered in BCT was covered in AIT—Advanced Individual Training.

AIT was the spray wax of the factory production line.

And the shiny new soldiers would roll off, ready for action.

Government Issue—GI.

71

FLOWER POWER

More than three decades later, I can't decide if the peace-love thing was born of Vietnam or was a response to it. Paisley and tie-dye guerillas sticking flowers into the muzzles of M-16s up in People's Park in San Francisco, a couple of hours above Fort Ord. Professional killers wearing symbols of dissent and pacifism into combat. It took irony to an art form back in 1968 and '69. Peace signs on helmets—the cryptic line drawing known in certain circles as "the footprint of the American chicken."

Make love not war! On the battlefield.

Most kids couldn't get a handle on the war that engulfed them, swept them up. Even those who wanted to believe and fight for something worthy.

Their cause and motivation always seemed like an incomplete sentence. Always requiring more questions.

And the answer to a simple, "Why?" might have been the complicated equation of a complex chemical reaction . . .

Or the dead silence of shame.

SAY IT LOUD!

Yeah! Yeah!

I'm black and I'm proud!

In 1968, James Brown declared on AM radio, they were black and proud.

The black soldiers would pass in the streets, on base, inside the barracks, meet and greet in the bowling alley, the PX,[*] or the mess halls.

Tap twice, clenched fists, and say, "Say it loud bro!"

It was cool not to finish the thing.

"Say it loud!" was sufficient.

The secret pact of a secret society.

Say it loud! Yeah! Yeah! I'm black and I'm proud!

It was a chink in the OD green armor of uniformity.

Where all things were the same, were identical, were GI.

Suddenly, they were black soldiers.

Not US or RA.

Not white soldiers.

Say it loud!

[*] *Post Exchange, the general store for military personnel*

FTA[*]

It was all over the base in 1968 and '69.

Penned in a quick, on-the-run scrawl.

Carved deeply into wood with a knife blade.

But the ink was disappearing—the carving would be puttied

in, painted over.

But below the surface you could faintly see a palimpsest

hieroglyph that couldn't be erased.

And then it would appear somewhere else.

On a wall, on a door, on a vehicle.

Ephemeral, yet indelible.

FTA.

* *Fuck the Army*

74

THE ABCs OF BCT

I was flipping through the Basic Combat Training manual
one day reading about how great the Claymore is.

The Claymore is an antipersonnel device.

Device is a euphemism for weapon.

It is an exploding mine containing shrapnel.

Personnel is a euphemism for human being.

Anti means against—hostile to.

Simple.

The Claymore is rectangular. About a foot long by ten inches
high, about five inches thick.

On the back it says BACK.

On the front it says FRONT—TOWARD ENEMY in raised block letters in the pot metal casing.

Simple.

The kind of ABCs covered in BCT.

SECURITY

US Government Property! No Trespassing! No Unauthorized Personnel! Restricted Area! Keep Out! Off Limits! The
signs were everywhere.

After living there a while, in Fort Ord, during the Vietnam
War, I was amazed to realize there was no real security there.
The fort was wide open.

The main entrance and the one on Tenth Street were the
two arteries that joined the fort to the real world outside the
fences and gates. Both had guardhouses with MPs monitor-
ing traffic coming and going. Going was easy, and coming
was no problem as long as you wore OD green.

If you did, the guard waved you in without hesitation. And if
you wore rank, he saluted and waved you in, in one unbroken
motion.

You could have quite literally moved an entire army into
Fort Ord in 1968 and '69—anyone's army. And they would
have been saluted and waved in.

That always amazed me.

HOLLYWOOD HAIR

The IG[*] Inspection! The Big Kahuna.

Happened only once a year—we prepared for weeks.

The whole fort had to be *Twilight Zone* perfect.

Pre-op sterile.

The whole fort.

I spent a week's pay on aerosol spray polish for my boots—which looked great if you stood perfectly still so it wouldn't crack and fall off in chunks.

The Inspector General was black. He wore Class As covered in pins and campaign ribbons. Gold braid. Black stripes down his trouser legs. His aides and subordinates were white. They all carried notebooks and pens, took copious notes. They were Lieutenants, Captains, and Majors.

We had to stand in front of our bunks with our lockers and foot-lockers open and on display. Beds made coin-bouncing tight. Standing tall. Looking clean, lean, and mean.

He finally got to me.

It was the same drill for everyone—everyone—over and over again.

He asked me what I did, by name, since it was printed on my fatigue shirt in black block letters. I tried to make it sound interesting. But it was pretty much the same as the other thirty thousand soldiers who lived there. We all did the same thing, pretty much.

He looked at my locker. All the stuff was hanging in the same

* *Inspector General*

direction. All the hanger hooks were facing the same way.

He pondered, then looked back at me and asked, "You from Hollywood, soldier?"

"Yes, sir," I said, trying to be friendly, yet still deferential. "How did you know?"

I really wondered. A heavy silence fell on the already silent barracks.

The General looked at me—the warrior elite.

He was probing my eyes for a spark of insolence.

He found none. I was from Hollywood.

He stepped back and said, "You got Hollywood hair, soldier. Look like a damned hippie. Get it cut A-SAP!"

I said, "Yes, sir." He moved on.

A subordinate wrote in a notebook that I had Hollywood hair.

TODAY

More than thirty years later, the fort is nearly empty. It would be empty but for a few small-fry entrepreneurs and a couple of bureaucratic annex offices—the Monterey Water Company, Jazzercize classes, horseback-riding lessons—all out past the hospital. Some of the land was given to California State University Monterey Bay. Someone's using a church. But other than that, so far, no one has had the imagination to put to use hundreds of acres and hundreds and hundreds of fully fitted buildings and structures that had been meticulously maintained by the hour for decades.

Fort Ord is a talus. A moraine left by a receding glacier.

Organized rubble in the wake of the Vietnam War.

It's already starting to disappear, with no one there to maintain it—turning to sand, like the dunes it was built on.

Being taken away by the onshore winds.

Cracks are showing in the blacktop of the streets and parade fields.

Flowers now grow with weeds as volunteers—RA, Regular Army. They both grow to nonregulation heights in areas once off-limits.

Sights, smells, sounds blow away as spores, to seed somewhere else—

In some other time.

But the wars never end for those who fought them.

And the memories blow forever through the empty barracks of the mind.

78

MORE GRAFFITI

The grand forces that move men across their own lives are today pushing Ord off the stage and away. The pace is accelerating, for it will soon be completely gone. And what will be left in its absence, regardless of its replacement? What effect, after all did it have on those touched by its existence? What was the sum of its being on the grand scale?

Life outside the old, disintegrating fort goes on pretty much the same as it always has. Yet for decades (and now decades ago) a lot of young men and many young women gave us their youth, their lives, or both for the shadow of a promise: Never again!

But they, too, were robbed of their prize, and their legacy is a treadmill through time.

And today, the aerosol torch is again carried by the children and grandchildren of America's warriors. Tattooed and pierced protestors spray their cryptic, caustic dissatisfaction on cold concrete inside empty meat lockers in silent, tomblike darkness. They gather and huddle by candlelight, as a secret society, to divine the meaning of crop circles, of ancient prophecies, and of war. They sit on the philosopher's stone in the very bowels of the dead fort and mix the elixir of life. They agree and decry, and rant and chant, adorn the cold hard walls with axioms, platitudes, and prayers . . . To no avail.

For they are as naïve as those who went before them. They leave behind the elements of their alchemy: rolling papers, broken bottles, and empty aerosol paint cans. And the ozone hole grows larger, outside in the sky above, as they, too, are pushed across their own lives, unaware of the grand forces that move them ever closer to their own destiny.

79

TIME TRAVEL

I drove up to Ord from LA in a pickup truck, a bicycle in the back, a camera around my neck, and took a ride through time, shooting these photos, writing these lines.

It's a different century now.

The old fort's foundations disintegrating, it seems to float, suspended in space and time, no longer held down by purpose.

The very atmosphere is thick with the energy of spirits, those souls who came before and came after I was there.

I can see them, smell them, hear them—their songs and cries, their threats, their bravado and their laughter.

The olive drab bodies marching, olive drab equipment rolling.

Polish and precision, endless maintenance.

The hustle and bustle of a war machine in high gear.

Now only in my mind's eye.

Silence and the singing of seabirds lay like a veil over it all.

The silent flight of a barn owl leaving the decaying rafters of a collapsing building to hunt the vacant grounds.

Weeds and wildflowers pushing up through the vast untended grave of the fort itself, already turning to dust before me.

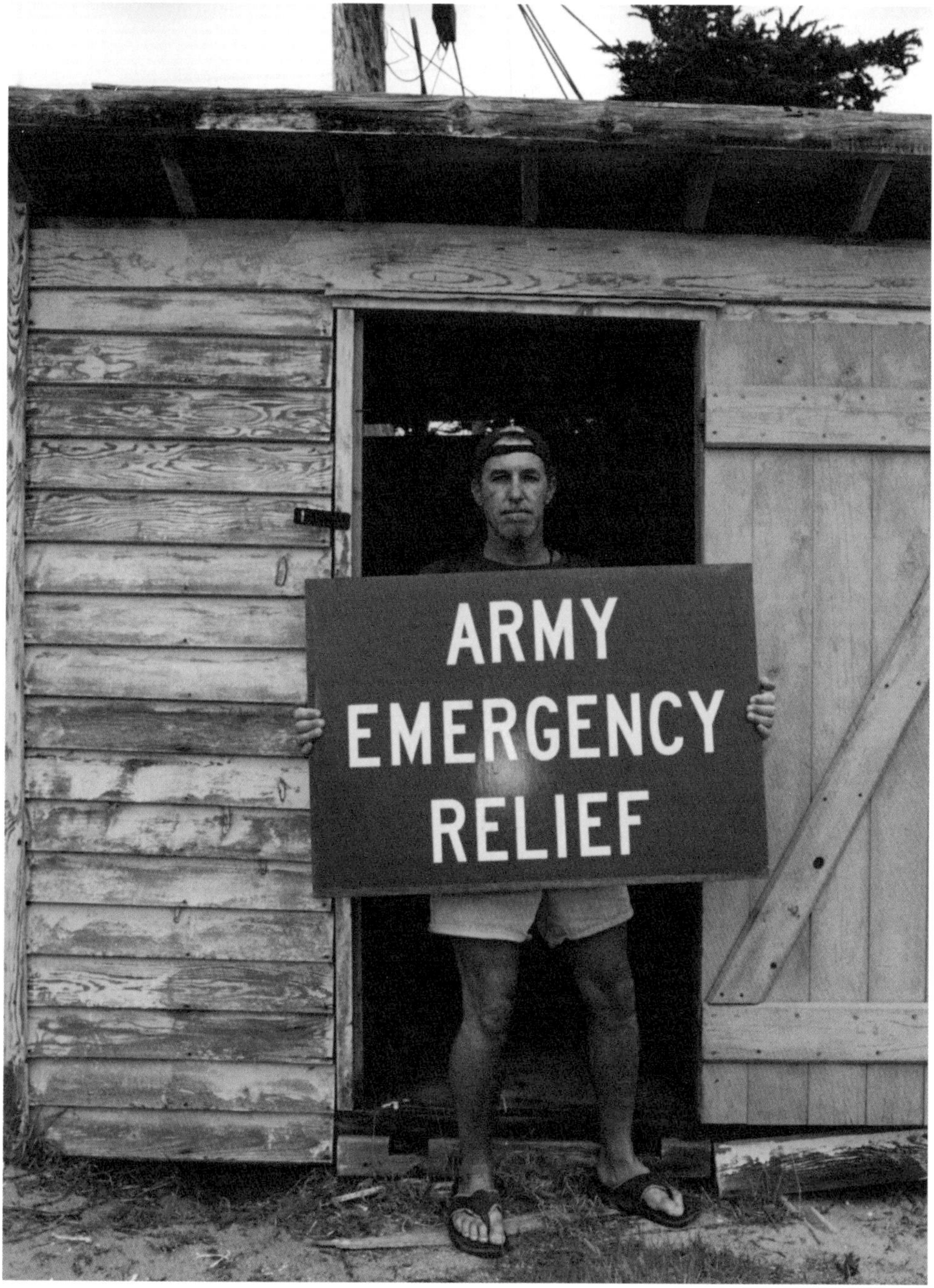
ARMY
EMERGENCY
RELIEF

80

NOT FADE AWAY

As I was last leaving the base, out on Highway 1, I drove past what was once a coyote on the roadside, under the huge green sign that says: Fort Ord—Main Gate.

The thin, fur-covered hide looked like burlap. It was dun colored, like all the tough weedy growth surrounding it. It's dead! I first thought, wrongly. For I could see it was already returning to the sandy shore in a transcendental state. The daily westerly winds were blowing it back as mineral-rich dust across the native succulents and coastal grasses that are home to lizards, snakes, ground squirrels, and mice the coyote had hunted and scavenged. And in turn these things live on the crawling bugs, flying insects, and worms that are sustained by the same coastal succulents and tough grasses that run along the shore to the north and to the south. The coyote was in a cycle of life unbroken by time.

And high above this subtle drama loomed a huge sandy dune, drifted proudly one hundred feet high. It was a soft terracotta color and totally barren except for a living sign written across the sand, high up near the top. It was in fact a declaration of love. It was written in the living, transplanted cuttings of native ice plants that had taken hold, rooted, and even flowered in the harsh environment of the dune above the highway.

It read: Matt loves . . . (the symbol of a heart signified the word). It was followed by several Asian characters connecting Matt's name with the heart. It was the name of Matt's precious love, written in life in the terracotta sand for all to see as they passed by on the highway below, where there used to be a fort called Ord, beside the blue bay of Monterey.

81

AN EPILOGUE

The big gears are turning still.
Cogs change, yet remain the same.
In 1968 and '69 our fashion statement was OD green.
The entire Army was awash in olive drab.
It had a smell to it: canvas and gun oil.
Then it started to change color. Inexorably.
The prism of politics held to a rising sun of war on the horizon produced the color, beige.

Years before Desert Storm and Desert Fox—campaigns and actions that sounded as though Madison Avenue had designed their marketing and acceptability, their logos—producing T-shirts, coffee mugs, flags, and the color beige . . .

Vietnam had almost no acceptability, but decades later OD green reached boutique windows on Rodeo Drive as a fashion statement. Fatigue jackets and caps, phony ranks and unit patches sewn on in silver and gold sequins.

The canvas and gun-oil smell was replaced by Chanel No. 5. Bleached blondes in convertibles would race through the streets of Beverly Hills as captains, or colonels, or sergeants on a shopping spree, dressed in the camp, flashy trash from the battlefields of yesteryear—Purple Hearts and diamond rings. OD green.

The new Army was beige.

Years before the wars in the desert.

Years.

The alchemy of the military turns rice into sand and lead into gold.

And the big gears are turning still . . .

In Enduring Freedom.

It was on my third visit to Fort Ord while working on this book that I happened upon the paintings. I was riding my bike through yet another seemingly endless geometric arrangement of rows and rows of misshapen two-story barracks when suddenly a sunlit gallery of vibrantly colored faces appeared before me. Their haunting eyes followed me as I approached. It was a magnificent display that stopped me short.

Dozens of acrylic paintings on Tyvek (a paperlike material used in construction) cover the windows of three or four barracks. I learned later that they were done by students from two local schools, California State University at Monterey Bay and Monterey Peninsula Community College. The Visual and Public Art program at CSU Monteray Bay organized the project (called, coincidentally, "Windows") in 1994, the year that Fort Ord was officially closed and part of its land given to the university for the opening of the school. The paintings, designed from the start to be window covers for the abandoned barracks, were done over the next couple of years and are based on family and archival photographs as well as interviews with military families.

Barely protected from the elements by the barracks' shingled eaves, the paintings are already vanishing. Most are gone, in fact. Some hang threadbare, shredded by onshore winds, others have been cut out and taken away in fits of fancy or vandalism. Yet still the paintings speak to us.

I saw instantly that these paintings are as much a part of the fort as any of the fading battalion shields, brigade badges, and company crests painted on walls and monuments

159

across the base. These faces are the embodiment of all those military logos—two sides of the same coin. The portraits cry out with individuality within the uniformed ranks, inspiring recognition and tribute, even gratitude. A statement of commitment posted for those who take the time to see.